Tame Your Emotions

Understand Your Fears, Handle Your Insecurities,
Get Stress-Proof, And Become Adaptable

By Zoe McKey

Communication Coach and Social Development Trainer

zoemckey@gmail.com
www.zoemckey.com

Copyright © 2018 by Zoe McKey. All rights reserved.

No part of this publication may be reproduced, stored in a retrieval system, or transmitted in any form or by any means, electronic, mechanical, photocopying, recording, scanning or otherwise, except as permitted under Section 107 or 108 of the 1976 United States Copyright Act, without the prior written permission of the author.

Limit of Liability/ Disclaimer of Warranty: The author makes no representations or warranties with respect to the accuracy or completeness of the contents of this work and specifically disclaims all warranties, including without limitation warranties of fitness for a particular purpose. No warranty may be created or extended by sales or promotional materials. The advice and recipes contained herein may not be suitable for everyone. This work is sold with the understanding that the author is not engaged in rendering medical, legal or other professional advice or services. If professional assistance is required, the services of a competent professional person should be sought. The author shall not be liable for damages arising herefrom. The fact that an individual, organization of website is referred to in this work as a citation and/or potential source of further information does not mean that the author endorses the information the individual, organization to website may provide or recommendations they/it may make. Further, readers should be aware that Internet websites listed in this work might have changed or disappeared between when this work was written and when it is read.

For general information on the products and services or to obtain technical support, please contact the author.

Thank you for choosing my book! I would like to show my appreciation for the trust you gave me by giving **FREE GIFTS** for you!

For more information visit www.zoemckey.com.

The checklist talks about *5 key elements of building self-confidence* and contains extra actionable worksheets with practice exercises for deeper learning.

Learn how to:

- Solve 80% of you self-esteem issues with one simple change
- Keep your confidence permanent without falling back to self-doubt
- Not fall into the trap of promising words
- Overcome anxiety
- Be confident among other people

The cheat sheet teaches you three key daily routine techniques to become more productive, have less stress in your life, and be more well-balanced. It also has a step-by-step sample sheet that you can fill in with your daily routines.

Discover how to:

- Overcome procrastination following 8 simple steps
- Become more organized
- Design your yearly, monthly, weekly and daily tasks in the most productive way.
- 3 easy tricks to level up your mornings

TABLE OF CONTENTS

INTRODUCTION 11

CHAPTER 1: EMOTIONAL INSECURITIES 23

CHAPTER 2: LOW SELF-CONFIDENCE 39

CHAPTER 3: INSECURITY................................... 53

CHAPTER 4: FEAR OF HUMILIATION AND
EMBARRASSMENT 69

CHAPTER 5: VULNERABILITY............................. 83

CHAPTER 6: DISCOURAGEMENT 93

CHAPTER 7: DISCURSIVE EMOTIONS 107

CHAPTER 8: HYPERSENSITIVITY 117

CLOSING THOUGHTS 133

REFERENCE 139

ENDNOTES... 141

Introduction

What are emotions?

The word emotion comes from the Latin *motere,* which means "to move." More precisely, if we stick the prefix "e" to the Latin word, it means to move away. Emotion, as a word, implies taking action. The most basic, instinctual emotions lead us to act or react to the external stimuli we experience.

Scientists have had a hard time discovering what's at the center of our emotions. Usually, we separate our rational mind, represented by the brain, and our emotional world, represented by the heart. There are lots of funny pictures about the struggle between these two and their fights on the Internet.

But, we know that our brain is responsible for our emotions too. More precisely, two little almond-shaped clusters called "amygdala," situated on either side of our brain. If we want to create a timeline, the hippocampus and amygdala were the two main components of our ancestors' brains. Later, through evolution, we developed the cortex and the neocortex. The amygdala is responsible for emotional memory. In fact, the amygdala is so involved in our emotional agenda that if it gets divided from the rest of the brain, that person won't be able to weigh the emotional value of anything.

If we feel that we're the victim of injustice, pain, fear, or danger, the amygdala reacts instantly, sending an alarm message to the rest of the brain. It's like the brain's security system, if an intruding intention gets to us, the amygdala starts howling, the danger zone's red lights start flashing and rotating, and all our lousy brainworkers get an emergency email sent to their computer. Depending on what kind of danger we face, the brain starts taking action.

For example, if we feel anger, we get a rush of adrenaline, the blood flows into our hands as we prepare to grab that stick and attack. Our heart beats like crazy, and in our mind, we picture steam coming from our ears like in old, clucking coffee machines. If we feel scared, the blood flows to our legs to make it easier to switch into flight mode, if necessary. Our face becomes colder, since most of the blood drained out of it to support our legs. That's why we get that chilly feeling when we're afraid of something. Our body releases hormones to turn our high-alert mode on and enhance our ability to make the best decisions for our safety.

When we are in love, for example, our brain sends a message opposite of fear and anger. We feel generally relaxed, sexually satisfied, and we would rather not separate from the subject of our love ever, ever, ever.

The aforementioned hippocampus is responsible for remembering facts and events. The amygdala remembers emotions related to these facts. For example, the hippocampus recognizes your spouse and the amygdala tells you that you love him or her.

On the land of the irrational

We often talk about emotions as being the land of the irrational. More often than not, it is a challenge to try to explain why we feel as we do. How often do we hear or think things like: *But it makes no sense. You have no reason to feel like this. Where did this emotional reaction come from?* We can feel weird and misunderstood at the same time because we can't understand why we react a certain way. However, we feel offended if someone questions the legitimacy of our feelings.

Has this happened to you? You felt okay, but then suddenly, for no apparent reason, you became tense and reacted with an emotional outburst to a seemingly innocent remark. And when somebody asked what was going on, you were unable to give a logical explanation. You just said, "I don't know, this is just how I feel."

I bet it happens more often than you realize. You think these emotions pop up, out of the blue, without a logical explanation. And meanwhile, they are difficult to sum up as a simple "you did this, so I felt that this and did that" equation.

There are always hidden reasons for why we react the way we do.

This book talks about the dark side of the emotional world. Why do we have negative emotions in different situations? I'm not a negativist, but let's face it, when we react positively, that's a blessing, we don't want to change that. We want to gain control of our negative, hurtful, and harsh emotions.

There is this saying, "think outside the box," but when it comes to understanding our emotions, the most important thing is to understand what is inside that box — our mind. The roots of different present reactions can be traced back years or even decades. Decades of misunderstood emotions can evolve into serious insecurities. This book will give you an easy to follow plan to learn, understand and balance your emotional confidence:

- What emotion do you feel?
- Why do you feel that emotion?
- How would your life benefit if you managed to understand the emotions in question?

- A step-by-step guide for how to learn to control or overcome emotional insecurity.

Klaus Scherer, an excellent psychologist, states that emotions are not only feelings, they are cognitive appraisals, physical symptoms, and action tendencies. To break this down, let me give you an example. [i]

Imagine yourself in a forest. Suddenly you hear a loud rustling in the bushes. To judge whether or not the noise represents a threat to you, you need a cognitive appraisal. You probably run some options — starting with things like wind or a fat bunny and working up to a vicious wolf or a bear — through your brain. Before deciding to activate the fight-or-flight response, you have to appraise the possibility of danger. It would be irrational to think of every possibility as scary, but also unwise to disregard every potential threat and pretend everything is fine.

Meanwhile, you identify the possible threat. You will probably experience some physical symptoms, as well, that are connected to the turbulent feeling you have because of the unclear nature of the disturbing stimulus. You may feel a rush of cold, a chill, sweating palms, verbal or nonverbal expressions, and a rapidly beating heart. These physical reactions are all the result of the perceived emotion of fear.

When your cognitive appraisal comes to the conclusion that you face danger, it activates the fight-or-flight response. You evaluate whether it is wiser to confront the danger or run to safety — this is what Scherer calls the action tendency. You might determine that since it's winter, the chances of the wolf being hungry are high. This means you don't have too much time to stay and think about what your most optimal course of action should be. You must react quickly to protect your safety as much as possible. Emotions can help you to choose a swift and effective action.

But what else made you able to put together this complex, emotional — cognitive — actionable response? Your memories and learned habits. In this case, you've learned to fear the hungry wolf; you *knew* it was dangerous, thanks to previous study. If you were a three-year-old without any knowledge of wolves being hungry in winter and lurking in the bushes, you wouldn't have had any reaction to the noise.

This means that some of the negative (and positive) emotional appraisals are defined by memories and theoretical or practical experience. The fight-or-flight response is instinctive, but the steps that lead to this reaction are based on experience.

This applies to other emotions too. So, going back to the problem of not being able to explain why you feel what you feel, there is always an unconscious series of events taking place in the background that lead you to emotional outburst, or as I will refer to it in this book, *emotional insecurity.*

Let's talk about an everyday example: pink is your favorite color. Once you heard your colleagues criticize this color, saying it was too childish for a grown woman to wear it. The remark wasn't addressed to you, it wasn't about you, but you still felt offended. You have two options:

A. you stand up for the rights of the color pink, zealously fighting for its recognition as a grown-up color (you choose to fight),
B. or you get up from your chair and resentfully move to another part of the office where you can't hear your colleagues, or just try very hard to ignore them while you feel upset (you choose to fly).

To explain this with Klaus Scherer's words, you heard something and after you ran through the cognitive appraisal phase, you concluded that it was in opposition with what you believe. You felt physical symptoms during the process, like a heavier heartbeat, a red fog that occupied your mind, and a desire to step up and retaliate for the injustice you had just suffered. If you are a more extraverted, gutsy person, your tendency will be to react more like point A. If you're an introverted, or shy person, your reaction will be more like B.

You might think, *Okay, that's a clear story, but it doesn't explain why I am offended when I evaluate the situation*. Good observation. The reason you react the way you do lies in your memories.

Anything you experienced in your early life that was discriminating, belittling, or judgmental plays its role in both reactions A and B. Which one will you live with? That depends how offended you are and on your temperament.

If you react as point A says, you feel entitled to your opinion and find it impossible to accept others' viewpoints because you take the remark about the color pink too personally. You feel the need to protect yourself against injustice. You're almost convinced that your colleagues were trying to offend you in a roundabout way.

If your reaction is more like option B, you handle the feelings of injustice, personal offense, and anger internally. You may not be brave enough to defend your position. You may think: *They consider me lame enough already*. You just want to escape or appear as neutral and oblivious as possible to make sure nobody will try to talk to you about the topic.

You may wonder why option A is a bad reaction. Standing up for ourselves and protecting our interests is a brave and useful quality. The problem is not with the reaction itself; sometimes, it is indeed a good way to go. For example, when you have clear proof of a direct offense you've suffered. Let's say your boss deliberately didn't pay your extra shifts, or someone told you, to your face, that you're a failure. ==In these cases, you should protect your boundaries and speak up. Although my example about criticizing the color pink is a bit silly, let's admit it — we often get mad and offended about the most trivial things.==

The problem with the reaction in point A is its oversensitive nature. It radiates a lack of confidence and insecurity. It is absolutely not certain that the insult was directed at us. But even if it was, so what? *Who cares? Who cares if they consider pink childish or feminine, and you are a man and you love it? Does the opinion of your colleagues about this color, or about what you should eat or wear, or the way you live, change the person you are? Do you really need their affirmation or acceptance?* You shouldn't give a flying... about your colleagues' loathing of the color pink. It doesn't change a thing. You still are the person beneath that pink shirt, and if you feel awesome in it, wear it with pride. And don't challenge your colleagues about their opinion. Just let it go. Don't throw rocks at every barking dog, because you'll never reach your destination.

The problem with point B is the lack of self-worth and too much dependence on others' opinions. If innocent or trivial things make you feel unhappy, you're facing a life full of sorrow. There are so many little displeasures around you that if you give power to each of them and take them personally, your life will be a jump race from one misery to the next. Most of the time these displeasures are not even about you. People mindlessly chatter about politics, and shopping hurdles, and preferred colors. More often than not they don't even think (about you or in general) when they chatter. So you shouldn't give too much thought either.

Reading this book, you'll be guided through common and less common emotional insecurities that can make your days bitter — how you can make peace with your fragile self, how you can avoid possessive behavior, how you can manage aggression or hypersensitivity, and many others.

Without further ado, please take the key to gaining emotional confidence and mindfulness.

Chapter 1: Emotional Insecurities

The story

Mr. Hare was not a social person. People would characterize him as a taciturn, but precise and hard-working man. Our leading character, after being heavily persuaded by his boss, attended the company's trimestral party. He felt very awkward during the event. He stood close to his colleagues, but not too close, of course; he didn't want the surprise of an unexpected question. He just stood close enough to hear what they were talking about.

After a while, he started feeling weird about his silence, and he decided to participate in the conversation. He spent a good five minutes listening to the ongoing chatter to make sure to say the right thing. He repeated his remark again and again in his head and analyzed how he should accentuate the words to make his point clear. When he felt the best moment has come to join, he took a deep breath and suddenly, timidly, rattled off two scattered sentences.

Deep silence followed. His colleagues looked bewildered. A female colleague gave him a half-grin and a small nod. And since he didn't go any closer, the group closed again and continued talking. Mr. Hare felt cold sweat running down his forehead. With a smile frozen on his face, he played a bit with his glass of sparkling water, nodding, looking around to determine who had seen his fatal fiasco.

> *What was I thinking? What just happened there? Did I say something stupid? For sure I did! Why? Why did I open my mouth? I knew this is going to happen!*

He heard laughter coming from the room he'd just left.

> *That's it! They're already laughing at my mistake! I can't bear it! How am I supposed to go to work tomorrow? Oh, I wish I could sink into the floor and disappear!*

The problem

Emotional insecurity is a feeling of general distress that is triggered when we perceive ourselves to be inferior or inept in some way. Whenever a person with low self-esteem, like Mr. Hare, does or says something that, afterwards, he considers stupid, off-target, or inappropriate, he feels immediate and deep remorse, anxiety, embarrassment, and devastation. His cheeks and ears turn red, he starts sweating heavily, and he wants to disappear from the face of the Earth.

He might escape from the place where the unfortunate event happened without saying anything, or become totally mute, hiding in the corner, hoping not to be noticed. In the following days, he may fake illness to avoid the people who saw his shame because he is sure everybody is thinking badly of him and laughing at him.

This deep-seated lack of self-esteem may last for minutes, hours, or days during which he will harshly criticize himself, and will be terrified of seeing anyone who was present when he made his mistake. Long or repeated shorter occasions of this kind can lead to serious depression.

More often than not, people like Mr. Hare have a self-made definition of good and bad (good or bad conversations, answers, hobbies, qualities, etc.), and they stick to it. They perceive the world through these definitions and make judgments based on them. However, their good/bad definitions usually are not realistic since they are strongly fed by insecurities and unrealistic expectations. And defining success based on unrealistic expectations is not doing them any favors.

The benefits of emotional confidence

People with high levels of emotional confidence never stop believing in themselves. Those who love and understand themselves — who aren't afraid to be who they really are — rarely feel insecure. They know they amount to their own self-worth, not a shilling more. And if someone's opinion is in opposition with theirs, it doesn't affect them. They accept it. They don't have to agree on it, though.

This is a big world. None of us are identical; we all have differences. It's unavoidable. This is why we should do our best not to be affected by differing opinions, because if we do, we'll be affected at every turn.

The solution

The problem with emotional insecurities in general is that people get too caught up in their own worlds — in those self-made definitions of good and bad I talked about. In order to rephrase these definitions, first one has to get distance from them.

How?

By becoming aware of them and consciously changing them. Easier said than done, true. But when it comes to understanding emotions, there is no easy way.

Russ Harris, the author of *The Confidence Gap,* explores a great mindfulness skill called defusion.[ii] Let me explain it a bit:

Defusion is the ability to get separated from your thoughts, or letting your thoughts flow freely without being affected by them. You simply don't allow negative emotions to hurt you. You don't *identify* with the negative thought.

Your head is like a nonstop radio; it will chatter and send new ideas every minute. But with practice, you can turn this loud radio into nearly silent background noise. As the saying goes, an entire ocean can't sink a ship if the water doesn't get inside. All the negativity in the world can't bring you down, unless you allow it to.

Mr. Hare was overstressed by other people's judgment. When he spoke up he radiated insecurity and by the silence he automatically thought he said something stupid. Maybe people were just surprised to hear his voice and didn't want to interrupt him. But, even if he had said something weird and had followed it up with a self-depreciating joke like, "Anyway I just wanted to get inside your secret society," and participated more actively in the conversation, then all the awkwardness of his previous mismatched sentence would have vanished.

People take themselves too seriously and often throw themselves a pity party if they mess something up. They often get hooked on their high expectations — their mind is throwing out one fear after another like an old radio, prompting them to take the bait. And when they bite, there's no easy way out — they get tangled in the deep pits of emotional insecurities.

It's like in the Disney movie *Hercules*, when Hades falls into the pit of dead souls. These sad souls jump on him as one, dragging him lower and lower.

What are the hooks or traps of the mind? (More specifically than negative emotions or emotional insecurities.) I called them the 4Fs, or the four fears:

- fear of obstacles
- fear of judgment
- fear of comparison
- fear of the future

The 4Fs can be helpful tools or killers of success. Let's look at each of them:

Fear of obstacles: It is only natural to encounter some obstacles when we are trying to accomplish something. When we evaluate the obstacles lying ahead of us in a critical manner, our mind proves to be quite an Einstein at solving the problem. For example, if we have to complete a task earlier than expected and we perceive the shortage of time as what it is — a shortage of time — our mind will work out how to compensate for the lack of time by becoming more focused and figuring out where can we save time — by skipping the gym, not watching TV, or wasting time on the Internet, for instance. In the end, we'll be able to finish our task.

But if we perceive the obstacle in a non-constructive way and we start panicking about it instead of looking for a practical solution, we'll waste time with worrying, OMGs, and blaming whoever cut our deadline. In the end, we won't finish what we need to.

Fear of judgment: Judgment is part of life. We judge during everyday situations without even noticing it. When we choose a cab, a place to eat, someone to date, or do business with — or quite the opposite, not to take any of these actions — we use our judgment.

When it comes to self-judgment, it is good to use critical thinking and point out real areas where we need to improve. For example, *I'm not so good at initiating conversations with people; therefore I'd like to learn and rehearse some lines, which could be handy*, is a fair statement. But when it becomes a self-punishing indictment like, *I'm such an unsociable, lame moron. I can't talk normally to people, I just freeze and blab, I will never get better at this*, it will produce the opposite results from what we expect.

Reinforcing our insecurity with negative affirmations will lead us into the Hades-hole — just falling deeper into it. What can you do? Be critical with yourself in a constructive way. Be critical about your self-criticism. Whenever your brain spills out something like the negative example above, ask yourself, *Is this really true? Am I really a lame moron who can't improve? Did I try to improve in the past six weeks? If so, how? If I didn't do anything to improve, why do I expect improvement? How can I improve?* Questions like these can give you a clearer image of what and how you need to improve.

Discard your fear of what others might say or think. It has no power over you, as long as you don't allow it to. If you feel this is not a strong-enough reason to leave your fears behind, do the same thing you did with your self-degrading affirmations. Be critical, ask questions. *Should I really listen to this person's criticism? What will happen now that she criticized me? How will it affect my life? Does it have a real consequence? Am I too sensitive about her remark? If yes, why? What past experience does her negative comment trigger?* Think about the deeper reason behind your fears. Usually whatever triggers a negative reaction in you is not about the present issue.

Fear of comparison: This is another gem of self-sabotage when we empower its negative side. We tend to compare ourselves to two types of people — the ones who are less fortunate than us, to gain confidence, and to those who are more fortunate than us but thus we lose confidence.

If we have a healthy self-awareness, comparing ourselves to others will help us learn and grow into better people.

For example, if you think, *David Letterman is a much better conversationalist than I am. What type of questions does he ask to make his interviews so enjoyable? How did he learn to do that? What could I learn from him?* This is a good way of approaching comparison. But if you get stuck in the *others do it better, they cheat, and they got lucky, poor me* rut, your comparison is not of much use.

Whenever you feel pressured by comparison, try to harness the lessons you could learn from the person you've got compared to, if there are ~~ay~~ any. First, make sure that the message of the comparison is legit and applicable. *Is this person really a better creative thinker than I am? What can I learn from him to improve my creative thinking?* Don't let despair, jealousy, or a sense of inferiority cloud your judgment or poison your day. Whether or not the comparison is right, losing your right mind is not the good way to react.

Fear of the future: Our minds have evolved through centuries to predict and anticipate possible negative outcomes. Thus, when we think about the future, we expect something bad to

We know that good & bad happen. It's normal. You are not a radical negativist if you catch yourself pondering a disastrous future. Now that you are aware of your mind going to the dark side, ask the following questions: What are the odds that this possible bad event will happen? When you determine the highest realistic risk, make a plan for how to respond to this worst-case scenario. Thinking negatively is natural, but if you let these thoughts affect your day, it's not okay.

If you run through the solutions of the 4Fs again, you'll see that there's no rationalizing in any of them. Their solutions are found in simple, constructive answers to the *What can I do in this case?* question.

Steve Hayes, the author of *Acceptance and Commitment Therapy: An Experimental Approach to Behavior Change* came up with a multitude of methods on how to apply defusion and get rid of the emotionally insecure thoughts we have all the time.[iii]

1. The three-step thought technique (this is my name for it).

The point of this technique is to think about one of your most emotionally insecure thoughts. For example, *I'm good for nothing*.

> - When you make your negative statement, start repeating it to yourself and see how you feel about it. How does it feel to tell yourself that you're good for nothing?
>
> - The next step is to add the phrase *I'm having the thought that... I'm a good-for-nothing person.* Now repeat this sentence. Does it feel different?
>
> - The third step is to add *I notice* to the beginning of the sentence — *I notice I'm having the thought that I'm a good-for-nothing person.*

Do you feel the difference? Did you succeed in separating the self-judgment and bringing it to a neutral thinking territory? Try it with different self-judgments.

2. A negative lullaby

The point of this exercise is to change the voice you use when thinking negative and insecure thoughts. Use the same self-judgment as before, or pick a different one.

> - Just like in the previous exercise, start repeating your negative mantra to yourself and observe how you feel about it.
>
> - Now repeat it to the melody of Frank Sinatra's song, *My Way,* or Britney Spears', *Oops! I Did it Again.*

Yes, it is a bit hilarious, but it serves the purpose of defusion. If you feel like it, smile or laugh, sing it out loud, choose your favorite melody, and sing it to that one too. Our thoughts are just like lyrics — words.

3. Oscar nominee

This exercise is quite similar to the previous one. Pick the same or a different negative statement of self-talk.

> -Repeat it to yourself and observe how much impact it has on you.

- Now repeat the same self-judgment in a famous cartoon figure's voice. Mickey Mouse or Popeye? It's your choice.

The effect should be similar to the previous exercise. Hearing your thoughts in somebody else's voice will help you think differently about that thought.

Let's go back to the story earlier in this chapter. If Mr. Hare would have read this book, he could have just sung to himself, *Oops! I did it again/I talked weird from my heart/My colleagues looked weird/Oh, baby, baby*. It's not rocket science; it only depends on Mr. Hare having the willingness to change and practice.

Exercises for this chapter:

1. Today I identified my fear of an obstacle that I will commit to overcome:

   _____

2. Today I identified my fear of a judgment that I will commit to ignore:

   _____

3. Today I identified my fear of a comparison that I will commit to leave behind:

_____

4. Today I identified my fear of the future that I will commit to leave in the past:

_____

Chapter 2: Low Self-Confidence

Life presents everyone with challenges that test our skills and our confidence. Over time starting in childhood, we develop a self-image of our abilities to step up to those challenges. When we allow mistakes, failures and the opinions of others to degrade this self-image, we create a condition of low self-confidence. Low self-confidence can permeate our entire life, resulting in less success and happiness. ==Fortunately, low self-confidence is a learned thought process, meaning it can be unlearned.==

The story

Stephanie is a 23-year-old college graduate with a business degree. She works as a methods analyst in an engineering office for one of the large auto manufacturers. She feels out of her element as she has no engineering background, but has to interface with engineers regularly to document best practices. Some of the other methods analysts in her group work just enough to get by.

Others are aggressive and work hard. She is the only woman in the group.

Stephanie and her boss just completed her first annual review and it didn't go well. He told her that she isn't assertive enough, doesn't drive her assignments, and doesn't speak out enough in staff meetings. He told her that when he hired her, he had high expectations. He told her that he thinks she can show him a lot more and hopes she can find some confidence and pursue her assignments with authority.

Although very upset that she disappointed her boss, she recognizes that she has heard this before from her previous boss and from her father. She decides to make some big changes, but is not sure how to go about it.

The problem
Low self-confidence is a type of self-evaluation in which a person believes, generally, that the challenges of day-to-day life are beyond their abilities. A person with low self-confidence is frequently uncertain about decisions, afraid to be wrong, hesitant to act and overly nervous about

risk. We often confuse self-confidence with two other related terms.

- One is self-esteem, which is a person's evaluation of her own worth.
- Another is self-efficacy, which is the confidence one has that he can successfully complete a particular task (as opposed to the tasks life presents in general).

So, again, self-confidence is a person's general view of themselves about day-to-day living. As you can imagine, the concepts of these three "selfs" are connected. But, interestingly, it's possible to have great confidence in your ability to perform a particular task, like cooking a meal (self-efficacy) but low confidence in your ability to face life in general (self-confidence). And the reverse is also true. Someone might be generally confident in their abilities to deal with the challenges of tomorrow, but extremely insecure about a particular task, like giving a speech to a full auditorium. Self-confidence and self-esteem tend to move in concert with each other. A person with low self-confidence often has a poor view of their value.

You might ask: "How does a person get low self-confidence?" Although it can be complicated, psychologists believe that it develops when a child is very young. Parents, or other people important to a child, play a big role. Curiously, either an overly critical parent or an overly protective parent can lead a child to believe that he is not capable of solving problems which, over time, leads to low self-confidence. The impact of an early childhood with overly critical or overly protective parents carries over into a child's school experience, perhaps even reinforced by an overly critical teacher in grade school.

We often confuse shyness with low self-confidence; but they are not the same. Shyness is a personality trait that is characterized by embarrassment and awkwardness in social settings, particularly unfamiliar ones. There is evidence that shyness is related to genetics, environmental factors, and prenatal care. ==Shyness is an innate personality trait. Self-confidence is a mindset.== Although the two concepts often parallel each other, it is possible to be shy and self-confident, or to be brash and have low self-confidence. For example:

Sean is always the life of the party. Regardless of when he arrives or who he arrives with, he quickly circulates, joking with friends, introducing his companions, and meeting new people. He has a joke or an amusing story for each group of people he joins. He really enjoys connecting with everyone and feels like he messed up if the party winds down and he skipped someone.

People are relaxed around Sean since he is genuinely easy to be with and is always the one to fill in the gaps if conversations start to slow. His friends view him as being confident and personable. Inside, however, Sean does not have a lot of self-confidence. When he was very young, his father — a successful, self-made entrepreneur — was quite demanding and critical of him. Throughout his youth, Sean believed that he never once met his father's expectations. He has come to believe that he will never be very successful, has problems making decisions, and doesn't follow through for fear of making a mistake. While naturally gregarious, Sean overcompensates for his lack of self-confidence by seeking universal social approval.

Self-confidence level differences exist between individuals from very low to very high. Either extreme can be a problem. People with very low self-esteem often resist expressing their opinions, avoid risk, hesitate when confronted with something new, avoid learning, procrastinate, and lack commitment to their beliefs and decisions. Overly self-confident individuals can be ambivalent to their failures, blind to the downsides of their decisions, and too quick to act.

Self-confidence rises and falls throughout a person's life, varies with particular social environments and the demands of daily living. If you maintain middle to high levels of self-confidence while staying away from the extremes, you will experience benefits.

The benefits of high self-confidence

Psychologists have studied self-confidence and other forms of self-image extensively since the early 1960s. Although self-confidence and self-esteem are often viewed as separate dimensions of self-image, they are highly related. Researchers have found that high levels of self-confidence and self-esteem are associated with:

- Better mental health
- Better physical healing capabilities
- Richer social lives and greater ability to get along with other people
- Stronger coping skills and greater resistance to adversity
- Higher school performance including more focused learning and more curiosity
- Increased job satisfaction
- Happiness
- Less fear and anxiety
- More willingness to be proactive and create one's own future
- Less fear of risks

The solution

Your level of self-confidence is a reaction to a learned self-image. It isn't imposed upon you by others, and it isn't inherited. Also, you didn't arrive at your particular level of self-confidence over a period of weeks or months. You arrived at your level over a period of years starting with your experiences growing up, reinforcing it with your reaction to life's challenges right up through yesterday. The good news is that because it is learned, it can be changed.

Increase your self-awareness

A starting point for increasing self-confidence is to work on becoming more self-aware. Learn to recognize the symptoms and patterns of low self-confidence in yourself. Do any of the statements below apply to you?

- Do you procrastinate on decisions because you fear to make an error?
- Does it take you a long time to make a decision?
- Do you frequently ask for help making everyday decisions?
- Do you hesitate offering an opinion in a group setting?
- Are you extremely anxious about taking a risk or making a change?
- Are you easily convinced to change your mind?
- Do you resist learning something new?
- Do you often just go along with something even though you disagree?

If you can easily answer yes to some of these questions and believe that it is a pattern in your life, then you are probably struggling with low self-confidence. Now, keep in mind, we all go through cycles in our life when our self-confidence rises and falls based upon people and events around us. Recognize the cycles and the momentary lapses, but look for the overriding patterns and trends.

Get to the root

If the answers to the above questions help you to see that you have low self-confidence, choose one of the questions and probe a bit deeper. You can do this by asking yourself four or five repetitive "why" questions. For example:

Melanie realizes that she is highly resistive to learning something new, particularly at work, and sometimes even with friends. She recognizes that this is part of her low self-confidence.

She asks: "Why do I resist learning something new at work?"

She answers: "Is it because I will learn slowly?"

She then asks: "Why are you afraid?"

"Because I will look stupid."

"Why do you think you will look stupid?"

"Because on certain types of things, I need more time."

"Why?"

"Because I get nervous and don't want to make a mistake in front of people."

"Why?"

"I've always been that way."

Reexamine your thoughts

Take a hard look at your questions and answers. You will find negativity, past mistakes, negative judgments by other people, hurt feelings, grudges, and a focus on weaknesses. Invariably, low self-confidence is bound up in an overemphasis on the negative aspects of your past experiences.

Refocus on the positive

Take each observation from your reexamined thoughts and find a positive aspect to the experience or feeling by:

- Refusing to judge yourself when something happens beyond your control.
- Turning a mistake or failure into a learning experience.
- Being less concerned about how others perceive you.
- Forgiving yourself. You will make mistakes.
- Focusing on what you are really good at. Improving what you are not.
- Looking at you past goals and making sure they were realistic. Doing the same with future goals.

Change

Focus on the positive aspects of your experiences. You can only increase your level of self-confidence by taking a series of small, incremental steps. These steps don't have completely serious and difficult. They can also be easy and fun.

Try to feel better about yourself. Put on your best clothes and take a walk. Get some exercise. If you have a mess somewhere, clean it up. Pick something small that you have been putting off and just do it. Pick a small task and win at it. Then celebrate. Get outside of yourself. Help someone.

Go easier on yourself. When something negative happens to you (outside of your control), this is not a mistake. Learn from it and move on quickly. If you make a mistake, learn from it. Then let it go.

Set reasonable goals. Don't set yourself up to fail. Don't assume failure. Assume success and work for it. Focus on your own self-evaluation. Place less value on what others think of you. Think about your own values and beliefs. Stick with them.

Become more proactive. Look for ways to do or start things. Don't worry about making mistakes. Don't wait for others. Find a way around obstacles. Learn something new every day. Don't be afraid asking questions.

You can increase your self-confidence through a series of small cycles of self-awareness, followed by small steps during which you change your habit of viewing yourself negatively. Then construct positive thoughts, followed by positive behaviors.

Putting it together

Low self-confidence negatively impacts our lives in so many ways. Since it is a learned thought process, we can unlearn it by being more self-aware and analytical about our own thoughts and reactions to events around us. Then we can find the positive aspects of our disappointing experiences and practice making positive changes in our lives.

Exercises for this chapter:

1. Today I identified why I lack confidence:

   _____

2. Today I acted confidently, despite my limiting beliefs:

   _____

3. Today I felt proud of myself by taking this bold step:

Chapter 3: Insecurity

The Story

"Oh! Now is the appropriate time for you to come back home, knowing I'd be here waiting for you, huh? You just come and go as you wish, no remorse… No, no, no! You left me here to go be with some girl. That's it, yeah? How dare you? You're such a…" Samantha once nagged her boyfriend, who had car issues and was only able to get back home to her that early because he got help from a friend who drove by.

At some other time, she had snatched her boyfriend's phone out of his hands to see who he was chatting with because he was smiling at the screen while typing, like someone who had just found the perfect soulmate. Little did she know, however, that he was chatting with his sister, whose companionship he enjoys more than any other person's. They had also once gotten into a heated argument because Vaughn — her boyfriend — didn't make her a sandwich, even though she had resented the idea when he proposed it to her before going to the kitchen to make his.

Sam, a witty and beautiful lady, had always considered herself lucky to be with Vaughn — a handsome and intelligent guy with the kind of physique that made ladies shiver at the sight. She truly loved him and didn't want to lose him, and he felt the same, but she never assumed this. Anytime Vaughn spent more time than bargained for at his friends' or mom's, or any place whatsoever, she immediately thought he was with another lady, because she supposed she wasn't beautiful and smart enough for him or she wasn't this or that.

The kind of arguments that ensued after a supposed wrong between Vaughn and Sam could totally be avoided. Sam shouts at her boyfriend's slightest unpassionate idea or action to her only because she thinks he's cheating on her. She doesn't particularly care what could have possibly transpired that made her boyfriend act or talk the way he did. She just wants to get at him by any means necessary, because she assumes she isn't worth dying for like he is, and that men like

Vaughn mostly do not end up with someone like her.

Do you see the problems here?

Samantha feels insecure in her relationship with Vaughn because of her *inferiority complex*. She doesn't believe in herself. Low self-esteem has eaten up all the potential of peace and love in their relationship.

On a second note, the couple lacks honest communication. If Sam feels insecure about talking about her insecurity, Vaughn should be able to assure her of his good intentions toward her. Doing this will increase Sam's self-confidence and self-esteem while reducing how often Vaughn has to be in an argument.

The problem

"Inferiority complex" is a term coined by the psychoanalyst Alfred Adler. It defines the state of mind of people who often find themselves in the personal limbo of self-doubt, self-resentment, and other similar states. They are found mostly trying to get praise from people for something they've done or an idea they've tabled in a meeting, for instance. Anything short of adoption of their ideas brings their self-esteem into question, and unreasonable doubts and self-resentments ensue.

Fear and anxiety are the cornerstones of emotional insecurity. Oftentimes, it has its foundation in early life experiences — that period of time when people tend to create their relevance in the spheres of the world. Some may try to do something different and awesome, but in an unorthodox manner. If they mostly get discouragement, especially from people they hold in high esteem like their parents or a successful family member, they begin to feel the idea wasn't a good one after all, and they probably would never be able to come up with a better one. Hence, they grow into fearful and anxious adults, always on guard, disappointed, and expecting the worst.

In 2015, James Brookes — a psychologist at the University of Derby, United Kingdom — investigated people with inferiority complexes who are always striving for superiority, in terms of self-esteem, self-efficacy, and confidence in their ability to succeed. The study provides some insight as to what may be going on in the minds of insecure people. People with insecurity tend to question their self-worth. They may also try to use empathy to make others feel sorry for them, at which point you may begin to doubt your own self-worth. [iv]

Samantha feels insecure in her relationship with Vaughn and nags him constantly to make him feel she's perfectly playing her role of the girlfriend while he is failing in his part. This may, in turn, make Vaughn feel he has been the problem of their relationship all along and start seeing his girlfriend as the perfect relationship partner while he sees himself as a degenerate — insecurity may begin to set in. This attitude is often seen in people with inferiority complexes. They brag about how perfect they've been at a thing, they flaunt their little successes to make others question their own values, they complain about the perfection of things or people — nothing is ever good enough with them.

Insecurity is distressing and has a threatening impact on people's psyches. Some people might become reserved and silent while they deal with their fears inside themselves, then erupt like a volcano. Some other people can become extremely aggressive. Insecurity can also turn someone into a controlling person, which is a defensive psychological reaction.

If insecurity takes an extreme form, it can affect everything in a person's life. There is a possibility of it threatening a person's ability to make pragmatic decisions, to maintain ambition, to handle disappointments, or even learn from their mistakes.

They are not open to trying new things, improving their skills, and they lose the ability to be introspective because they hold themselves to a difficult and practically unattainable set of self-assessment criteria — we all hate to be second-guessed.

How to Manage an Insecure, Possessive Partner

Remember the cause of Samantha's problems with Vaughn? Let's focus on Samantha's inferiority complex, which brings about her insecurity and lack of honest communication between the couple. The very factors that point out insecurity in a partner are the same ones that guide us to the solution.

A romantic partner might feel threatened and insecure in a relationship for a number of reasons, including disapproval sustained during childhood and low self-esteem. This may lead such partners to become overprotective and possessive. He or she may want to be with you all the time because they fear losing you. And because a supposed inability and low confidence to get another romantic partner that'd be affectionate. As such, an insecure partner may tend to behave as though he or she owns you and must have access to every nook and cranny of your life.

If you feel your partner acts possessively, sit him or her down and make it understood how you feel when they act possessively. Some people may not be aware of their inappropriate behavior, and as a result, you need to subtle in this discussion so as not to enflame their insecurity.

Don't attack them, and don't make it personal. Tell them, "I feel sad when you're acting possessively," not "I feel sad when you're possessive." Carefully elucidate to them that there's nothing wrong with them as a person, and their behavior just needs improvement.

While in conversation with an insecure partner, try to listen attentively and be attuned to their person. They may attack you and tell you something that can make you doubt your own personality. Know that they do this mostly out of anxiety, not with the sole purpose to hurt you. When they tell you things like you don't love them, try not to become defensive, but listen and reassure them both in words and in deeds that you love them dearly. Speak you mind with confidence, but be conscious of their person and choose your words carefully so as not to hurt them.

You are not trying to cajole them; you're trying to make them feel secure in the relationship and help increase their level of self-worth and self-confidence.

Act as described above a few times. However, don't forget to protect your boundaries. Describe the behaviors and situations you are not willing to tolerate. Bring up only those things you are not willing to compromise on like, "Samantha, I don't accept you snatching my phone from me and searching through it," and "I don't like it when you make me feel guilty. Please stop saying things like this or that." Be specific.

Possessive behavior is a sign of low self-confidence and inadequacy. Assure your partner that you are determined to be by his or her side. Stand by those words once you utter them. If you know it wouldn't be possible for you, don't mention it at all, because when you do and you fail to adhere, you only breed more doubts in your partner. First, make sure you are willing to persist and not leave after a month.

However positive and helpful it may sound, it doesn't mean you have to sacrifice your entire life just to reassure your insecure partner. Have a conceptual deadline with milestones in your head. Don't start with ultimatums. For example, if you need to reassure you partner about your love each week, and after a few months he or she no longer thrives on the weekly reassurance, but prefers it to be monthly, we can call that an improvement. However, if after a year he or she still needs weekly reassurance, it means there is no improvement, which is not okay.

If the latter is the case, it is time to talk about your problems — again. Tell your partner how the constant reassurance of your love to him or her makes you feel. Tell him or her you did what you could for a year, but things haven't yet improved. You can even ask them what they would do in your place.

If you feel that the relationship has become toxic as a result of your partner's repeated possessive, insecure behavior, it's time to consider leaving the relationship. If you spent time trying to make things better — even counseling — without the desired results, it's time to put your own interests and wellbeing before anything else.

Breakups don't happened easily; they come with plenty attempts at emotional blackmail. Once you're certain about your decision to end a romantic relationship, don't let empathy draw you back in.

How to Personally Overcome Your Insecurity

Many insecure people live a "security in obscurity" lifestyle. They don't want to accept their insecurity, even when they know how vehemently it affects their life. The first way to get a solution to any problem is to first admit the existence of a problem. I must emphasize how bold of a leap is to accept your insecurity. This is the beginning of the solution to your challenges.

Some emotional insecurities are rooted in your early childhood experiences — maybe you lacked parental love and guidance, or the kind of parental love you were exposed to was inadequate, or you got scolded when you should have been praised. However, all those happened during your childhood, and you're no child anymore. You are in control of your own life. You determine whether to take the hill or take the plain. You can consciously change and shape your life to that personality you've always admired.

To start, ask yourself the following questions and possibly voice them, or write them down:

- Why do you feel insecure?
- What is the reason you feel the need to act the way you do?
- What are you afraid of?
- Why do you think you are not enough?

Once you've done this, you'll be able to know where you insecurity is coming from and how you can ward it off. You'll have a good grasp of what makes you feel insecure and why. With this knowledge, you can either avoid those things or stand up to them. If you feel insecure about being able to identify your insecurities, ask for the help of a specialist. You don't necessarily have to make talking to a counselor a regularity in your life. Just make sure you have guidance on how to handle your insecurities.

I don't recommend involving a friend or relative in this matter. They can be biased or overprotective. You need objective opinion about your issues.

If you conclude you have certain shortcomings that need to be changed, make a persistent effort to change them. If, for instance, you get upset at seeing your colleague at work do better than you and get more praise than you do, don't let it get to you, but let it be a motivator for you to also perform excellently. Don't do this for the praise, but for your peace of mind. Whenever you make an effort to improve, analyze your whys. If we take this example as a basis, doubling your efforts at your workplace to grow personally is a good motivation. Doing the same to impress someone, or defeat your colleague, won't help you with your problem. Redoubling your efforts will give you a sense of accomplishment in the short-term, but when your colleague passes you again, you'll fall back to the pit of your inferiority complex.

You are in competition only with yourself. Remember that your life is not the same as that of your colleague's. You're in no way insignificant at your workplace, because you contribute that seemingly little quota of yours to the general development and sustainability of your organization. Know that each brick is needed in the wall.

Speak aloud whatever rational solution you've written for the problems you've highlighted earlier. What you say about yourself is what you become. It will benefit everyone, especially you. Just like insecurity didn't jump at you suddenly, this change won't happen overnight, either. It takes time, but don't think it isn't worth your time. Eventually, you will feel the change in your actions and self-picture.

You have to leave the past behind you. Let what happened during your childhood stay with your childhood. Let whatever transpired between you and your previous partner stay between you and that partner. Don't carry over the negativities of your past into your present. Your past is gone — learn from it, but focus on today and tomorrow, because this is what you have.

Maybe you were fooled, cheated on, and you lost faith in people. It's a normal emotional reaction. If you rationally examine your past when you were cheated on, you'll realize that it is not your current partner who cheated. You shouldn't punish him or her for someone else's mistakes. It is no general inference that if one man or woman cheated, then all men and women will do the same. Do not let the previous bad experience ruin your present chance for happiness.

Know that the more you pressure someone with your doubt and possessiveness, the further you will push them away. Your actions may result in your current partner committing something similar to what your previous partner did because you pushed them to desperation with the same bad behavior. Recognize the pattern and avoid making the same mistakes.

If your partner does something and you want to react to it, take enough time to carefully analyze your reaction and envision the possible outcome. Put yourself in his or her shoes and with an open mind, think of how you'll feel if it were you and with this consciousness, move forward with or deter your supposed reaction.

If each of your partners ends up doing the same thing to you, there must be something you do wrong, too. Try to figure what your mistake is and correct it. If it will help, you can use a journal to document this.

Have your own life, let your partner live his, and when you are together share the best of both. Have your own work, hobbies, and social life. Do not spend all your time with your partner just to be able to keep an eye on him — that breeds insecurity. When you're without your partner, doing your own thing, don't let the thought of him with another man or woman come to you. If it does, respond to it with things like, "he loves me dearly and cheating on me won't even cross his mind; so, why worry?" Relationships are built on trust and you should learn to trust your partner whenever you are apart.

If you do things separately that you can share afterwards, you'll always be an interesting person. It is important to spend time together, but it is also fun if you spend time apart from each other and do different things you can share and talk about when you're together.

Exercises for this chapter:

1. Today I stood up against this type of aggression:

   _____

2. Today I discovered that I have this aggression pattern in my behavior:

   _____

3. Today I decided to consciously fight against my aggressive behavior:

Chapter 4: Fear of Humiliation and Embarrassment

The Story

Josh got an invitation from his friend, Brad, to celebrate his baby's first birthday with his family and close friends. Although he was very pleased by his friend's thoughtfulness, Josh felt a growing anxiety. Josh was naturally not very outgoing and mostly doesn't feel socially secure. About a year before this invitation, when Brad's kid was born, Brad had organized a get-together of a small group of friends — of which Josh was one — to celebrate the birth of his son. Josh had a bit more than usual to drink during the get-together and had tried to pick up Brad's sister, Jessica, who publicly rejected him.

Ever since this incident, Josh hasn't hung out with his friends. He has rarely spoken with Brad, and has been telling himself that he only doesn't want to bother Brad because of the baby. Josh has lived the past few months in a state of deep lethargy and isolation, because whenever he bumped into one on his friends who was present at the party, he immediately recalled the incident and started to feel he was in the spotlight of ridicule. He was convinced everybody was still talking about his shame from the baby shower and often ruminates over it.

Josh doesn't want to face the same people, especially Jessica, again. What if someone brings up last year's rejection? Ugh, he'd be so humiliated. So why take the risk? He has been deprived social security by embarrassment and fear of humiliation from one year ago, and he's yet to get over it.

Oftentimes, people claim to be humiliated when what they've actually experienced is embarrassment, or vice-versa. As such, it is important to differentiate between what embarrassment entails and what comes with humiliation.

The Difference Between Humiliation and Embarrassment

Embarrassment and humiliation both stem from the judgment of another person on what a victim has said or done. Unlike shame or guilt that is self-infused, they both come from what one or more third party(ies) does or say about a victim's action. As much as embarrassment and humiliation find their roots in the same ground, they differ slightly from each other.

Embarrassment is brought upon oneself. You do something that isn't generally acceptable and you feel distressed about it, but you can deal with it because you personally admit the fact that whatever you did wasn't right. You're the judge of your own behavior. Josh had too much to drink, went to his room, threw up a couple times, and went to sleep. He wakes up to see the mess he had made, feels embarrassed about it, and cleans up; all good, nothing spoiled.

Humiliation, on the other hand, is brought upon someone by a third party. It may be a private or a public rejection, or denial. Josh — a socially insecure person — had too much to drink, walked up to Jessica, whom he had been eying for a while, and acted drunkenly by trying to kiss her. Jessica, instead, slapped his cheek, bringing attention on the duo. Josh would have just felt embarrassed if Jessica had blocked the kiss, but now he feels humiliation because Jessica has brought the eyes and ears of others onto their private affair.

Humiliations are more difficult to get over, unlike embarrassment. The more time passes over an embarrassing situation, you tend to remember it less and less. Humiliation, however, digs a well of ordeal inside a victim and stirs it up when the victim comes across any element of remembrance of their humiliating experience. We may brood over the experience for months, or even years, and become obsessed with revenge against the perpetuators of the humiliation.

Now that we've established some basic differences between humiliation and embarrassment, it'd be easier to focus on the cause of the problem and propose a solution without conflating the two terms.

The Mystery Behind the Fear of Humiliation

The fear of humiliation and embarrassment causes a person's private or public status to be undermined. Humiliation is an assertion of power to destroy or deny a person's status quo. It undermines a victim's defensive ability against antagonists. A person who, for instance, speaks against prostitution but gets caught in the act won't have the audacity to encourage people to stay away from prostitution. Whether or not such person's mischievous act was publicized, the confidence to preach against prostitution has been soiled, just as Josh's value after Jessica humiliated him has been tarnished.

Humiliation has been used as a form of punishment against violators of the law from the beginning of time. It was used by elites in the early centuries to main order and uphold honor among the people. The thought of being humiliated for a traditionally wrong act made people abstain from such acts and kept peace and harmony throughout different cities.

Violence is oftentimes attributed with humiliation when humiliation may be passive and occur without violence. Snubbing a person or affording them lesser than their status quo demands is equivalent to humiliation. Betraying and blackmailing a person like what happened to Chris

Huhne — the British Secretary of States for Energy and Climate Change in 2010, who was betrayed and humiliated by his ex-wife — brings humiliation that can't be more tarnishing to such person.

Although, violence may not accompany an act of humiliation, the victim of the act may react in anger and hostility. In many other cases, the victim may be traumatized with fear and anxiety, social isolation, sleeplessness, apathy, depression and suicidal inclination. [v]

Humans have different tolerance ranges. As a result, the amount of humiliation one person can bear may be too much to bear for another, given the circumstances surrounding the situation like how many people might mock the person or what it does to the person's reputation, as in the case of Huhne. In the case of severe humiliation, death is often considered a better option than soiling one's reputation — something similar to dying with some sense of dignity.

People who suffer humiliation and are remembered for it can experience life as a real drag. When people see them along the street and want to use them as a reference in a discussion, they'd say things like, "Isn't that the guy that was slapped at a party for trying to kiss a lady?" or "Remember that lady that was stripped naked for walk of shame in the *Game of Thrones* TV show?" etc. It is hard to swallow such public attention. (When I say public, it can be as much a handful of people or the entire world, depending how well-known the "hot topic" is.)

Humiliation is mostly accompanied by shame, but not always. A victim may be humiliated and publicly disgraced, but it is rare for someone to feel ashamed at their humiliation if they are highly socially secure and unwaveringly believe that what they've done is right.

Humiliation isn't a justified response to a disagreement or situation. Not even crimes. Why? Because it doesn't effect justice for any wrong whatsoever, but breeds hatred, anger, and revenge, which only increases crime rates.

If you've experienced or have faced humiliation, know that violence, anger, and revenge threats aren't the appropriate reactions to the situation, because they do nothing to reverse or repair the damage that has been inflicted on you. Instead, it is healthy to learn how to uphold or rebuild your self-esteem.

Five Ways to Overcome Humiliation

You're not alone; don't hide. Hardly does anyone pass through this world without suffering a form of humiliation. When I was in my early teenage years, my classmates used to mock me for being a good student and coming from a smaller, rural place. They drew pictures on the blackboard in the morning about me driving a tractor and reading a book. When I got to the class, they even chanted some weird, made-up tales about my "adventures" in my village and laughed heavily. Although the memory doesn't affect me at all today, I remember this event so clearly because it used to hurt a lot. I didn't have my parents around to stand up for me, so all I could do was retreat to the toilet until the class started and the teacher arrived.

The degree of humiliation can differ. There are others that have suffered similar, or even worse, humiliations than I have, and a number of them got over it. Were you bullied or humiliated? Don't be afraid or embarrassed to seek a support group that'd help you overcome your humiliation and encourage you to move on.

In life, success isn't completely dependent on talent, but on hard work and resilience. Many talented individuals are rolling in the depths of fear of humiliation, even if they haven't come close to actually experiencing these things. Humiliation, in whatever degree, may come, but it shouldn't limit your potential. Don't give up because you messed up the first time; be resilient.

Learn from your experiences. Experience is the best teacher, many say. If Thomas Edison hadn't learned from his 999 experiences to make a lightbulb, we probably will still be using gas lamps now. You have to check out your past humiliation experiences and combine them with the knowledge you have today to define your future.

Use your downtime to do things you enjoy. Instead of brooding over your humiliation, liven up. Do something you enjoy. See a movie, play video games, read a book, cook — anything! This way, the burden associated with a past humiliation won't settle in your mind.

See the crisis as an opportunity to grow, to get stronger, and move on. Most successful businesspeople have at one time utilized a period of crisis to make huge profit because they don't waste time wallowing in thoughts of how the crisis may affect their business. Similarly, see your humiliation as a way to be better at what you probably did wrong. Don't reel; move on and take advantage of the situation. Garner confidence to speak and ask that lady out on a date again, or whatever.

Five Ways to Deal with Embarrassment

Stop apologizing. People often try to apologize when they've done or said something embarrassing. Apologizing doesn't make you feel better, nor does it lift the embarrassment off your shoulders; it only makes it worse. The past is past. Your apology is no longer needed. Focus on the now.

Laugh about it. If you have been embarrassed, it is now in the past, and stories of such situations make for good jokes at a cocktail party or a get-together. Feel free to relay those embarrassing moments that makes ribs crack when people hear them. Don't be rigid and oversensitive about it; it is now in the past. Laugh it off with your friends and have a good time over it. When you do this, you'll feel less afflicted by whatever it may be.

Think about this: Your embarrassment is as a result of your imperfections. You have a standup comedy show to do, you've had all your lines well-rehearsed, and you've already defined your expectations from the audience. Unfortunately, the reactions from the audience were below your expectations, even though you had said and done all you planned to say and do, making you feel embarrassed. Truth is, you didn't tilt.

Not all situations live up to our expectations, and when they don't, rigidity isn't the perfect solution. Learn to compromise, but do it carefully without losing value. A therapist once said, *What we don't want to do is fall over, but when we never allow ourselves to tilt, we fall over.* Tilt mindfully.

Learn to handle fear. Taylor Clark, an author and a psychologist, said in an interview that we have the power to define how we relate to appalling emotions, even though we can't instantly stop ourselves from being startled at things that scare us. Embarrassment is the fear of being observed as less than who we think we are. The more we welcome and tackle fear and anxiety, the better we become at subduing embarrassments.

Visit your embarrassing past and solicit others' stories. Practice writing about your past embarrassing moments. This is not to well up the demeaning past, but to keep the future in check. For you to have been embarrassed, you must have done something below your own standard. Check for these things in your list and learn from them.

Solicit for stories of embarrassing moments from other people. When you get to see others', you might giggle, "Mine wasn't as bad as this," which in turn makes you feel better and also keeps you in check.

Remember, embarrassment and humiliation get a firm grip on you when you don't learn to demoralize them. They both present you with fear to cripple your potential, and in the case of humiliation, to keep fantasies of revenge against your humiliation perpetrators, thereby making the productive part of you inactive. Don't give a chance to that fear. Learn to live by it, learn to handle it, and learn to overcome its footholds with these few, but effective steps.

Exercises for this chapter:

1. Today I did this activity and it made me cheerful:

_____

2. Today I talked to this person, who encouraged me:

_____

3. Today I left this person behind because he or she discourages me all the time:

_____

Chapter 5: Vulnerability

The Story

Let's pretend you're playing truth or dare with your friends. You are nervous and self-conscious about choosing dare, as many of us are, because you don't want to do anything compromising or embarrassing. So you pick truth.

The person asking the question is in an emotional mood, so he asks you what you dislike about yourself the most. There are four people in the game, and you know three of them. But there is also a (nice) stranger. You start feeling uncomfortable. You really don't like to talk about your weaknesses in front of others. You like to maintain an image of yourself as somebody who is okay with herself, and who doesn't have anything she dislikes about herself.

Except your nose; your belly; your weird, ass-shaped chin; your manly fingernails; your pimples; your impatience and deep insecurity; your intense wish to belong and feel loved; your deep scars from previous relationships that still affect your present relationships… Oh, no, you cannot tell them all these things. What will happen to your image? What will happen if you attract even more attention to your Cleopatra nose or, even worse, what if they notice you actually care?

Is talking about your insecurities a weakness? Will you be considered weaker if you admit how much of a mess are you dealing with internally? Will you be judged or become a laughingstock? Will people lose faith in your secure and seemingly well-composed character?

But you have to tell the truth… This game is about truth, and you'd feel ashamed if you lied. So, you open your mouth, and with a shaky voice, awkwardly trying to find the right words, you pour everything out — the discontentment you feel toward yourself, the insecurities you carry, and everything that passed through your worried mind. It's out there. You're exposed and totally, utterly vulnerable.

These are actually my fear. This is my story. I'm a confidence coach, and I write about self-development, as you read at the beginning of my book, on my website, or social media account. Does this mean I am untouched by negativity? Not at all. I'm getting better at overcoming my own fears and at sharing the paths I've found to success with other people. I've had to become better at dealing with my own negative feelings.

But the truth is you cannot eliminate them forever. There is no magic solution that can eliminate fear, defeatism, or anxiety from the face of the Earth. But there are antidotes, like awareness and acceptance, and when you see a negative pattern starting, you can choose to fight it. I chose to fight the fear I felt when I was asked this question.

What will these successful American people think of me if they know? But then I asked myself this question: What will I think about myself if I don't take their curiosity seriously and don't answer them honestly?

So, I gave them my honest answer. You know what happened? I felt better. I felt proud for not preaching nonsense to my readers. I overcame my fear. I chose to be brave.

And you know what else happened? It turned out that one of the girls felt uncomfortable with her nose too. One of the guys made similar mistakes as I do when it comes to relationships. And the game turned into an honest exchange of opinions and experiences. I didn't feel alone with my problems, and I gave comfort to my friends too. After this big realization, we started talking about how we are all coping with negativity, and how we can give each other good tips. I still feel empowered by that evening.

And to push my vulnerability to the next level — I just put that experience in this book. And now you've read it, and know it. And you can relate to me, or you can be pissed that you just bought a book by someone who is dealing with negative stuff. I accept any opinion or judgment you have. This is the wonderful thing about embracing vulnerability: once you do it, you actually get rid of fear.

The problem

When we try to make others believe that we are not vulnerable, we lie. Everybody has that spot. But that lie automatically generates fear in us:

What if they figure it out? What if they judge my vulnerability and dishonesty?

So, you cause yourself additional fear. I'm pretty sure you lied to your parents about something when you were a kid, and then you were terrified about them discovering your lie. Or you lie to your partner about something, which is not exactly a white lie, or to your boss, or anybody... As soon as the lie leaves your mouth, you feel pressure — sometimes actively and sometimes passively.

And if you accumulate many lies, there's a greater chance that you'll forget about some of them, and one idle day, you'll accidentally reveal your own lie. And that's much worse than being honest about a weakness. I've become very abstract, so let me give you some examples of vulnerabilities you can lie about.

- When you apply for a job, you lie to your boss and say that you can handle stress very well. They hire you, but at the first busy closing period, you become irritated. Your system collapses, like Windows does when the entire screen goes blue, and nobody has any idea what the heck should be done. Impossible to turn off, impossible to restart

— brain dead. If there is an IT specialist, or in your case, a stress-handling mastermind, everything will be fine. But don't forget, you were hired to be the stress-handling mastermind.

If you were had honestly admitted that you are not good at dealing with pressure, you might not have gotten that job. But in the end it will be a win-win: The company finds somebody better for that position, and you don't get trapped in work you'll very soon hate.

- The first date syndrome — where everybody is so cool, so funny, and so good. "Relationship? No, I don't want to trap you. Just fun, fun, fun. Kids? I hate kids. I don't want kids from you. Don't worry, I'm not a needy type." How often do we lie to men to make them believe we are the woman they want us to be (based on our womanly judgment)? Or men, how often do you tell us women that you want emotions, that you love to spend time with your partner, and that you are very good at working out problems to make us believe we just met Prince Charming on his white... bicycle?

I'm pretty sure all of us have experienced both sides of the conversation — when you were telling more (or less) about who you really were, and then your date did. And in a few weeks or months, the surprises start to come. The woman starts insisting on a relationship where they live in a bubble. The guy starts forgetting the mushy words. Then you just sit, stare, and wonder who that other person really is.

I'm not saying you shouldn't try your best on a first date, but do not hide or lie about your core values because you think the other person wouldn't approve. Isn't it much better to just be who you are? If you're a good match, you'll be accepted anyway, and if not, isn't it better to know that now?

These are typical patterns when we want to appear less vulnerable. We want short-term happiness, so we lie.

The benefits of vulnerability

Peace of mind comes as soon as you realize how important it is to embrace it. Embrace who you are. You can always fine-tune those qualities you don't feel good about, but you can only do it well if you first decide to love yourself as you are in that imperfect, vulnerable, and exposed state.

If you always say you'll love yourself when you are the person you want to be, that day will never come. The correct chronology is acceptance, love, and then change. Not the other way around.

What's the benefit of embracing vulnerability? An honest life, where you don't have to fear judgment or that you'll be discovered because everything is already out there. And, perhaps it is hard to believe, but it will be your shield.

Being totally out there — accepting your goofy, mushy, picky, impatient, clumsy self — is the greatest power you have. In this state, you will be the closest you can be to unbreakable. Know that yes, you're already broken, so there's nothing to break anymore. You are a wonderful mosaic — a unique, colorful picture of your personality and emotional world.

The solution

This entire chapter was the fact, the problem, and the solution in one. I really didn't divide the flow into the shape you have become accustomed to in the previous chapters because vulnerability isn't really an emotional problem. It is emotional power, if you are willing to use it. True, it can also be a weakness. But it is only a weakness if you try to hide or deny it.

If you dare to open up, being vulnerable means that you're willing to open up to new experiences. Without vulnerability, it is hard to develop your ability to connect with others and to fully experience and accept yourself. People connect best through their vulnerabilities. I've experienced it myself.

Vulnerability indeed means being open to experiences, giving fear your middle finger, and accepting that things may not work out as you had hoped. Without it, as I said before, it is hard to be open to new things that are uncertain such as love, trust, friendship, and creativity.

Exercises for this chapter:

1. Today I embraced this vulnerability:

___

2. The vulnerability above is good and helps me because:

___

3. Today I helped this person with his or her vulnerabilities:

___

Chapter 6: Discouragement

The story

Grace, a fast learner and very intelligent lady, has been the receptionist of her medium-scale organization for quite some time now. She has seen many employees come and go, including top official personnel. In fact, she has almost become indispensable to the organization because of her warm customer service skills. She knows when a customer is bored or angry and controls whichever mood they came to her desk with — since she's the first person everyone meets at the entrance — and gets into their head well enough to quench anger or lighten up the mood, or any other appropriate thing to do. "Be thankful to your receptionist. I was going to bring hell to you before I met her," an angry customer had once told the manager upon getting to her office.

As witty as Grace may sound, she has her shortcomings — which eats a good deal of the potential up in her. For about four years now, she's been envying the seat of the manager of the organization, but she's always scared to make a move. Sometimes, when she's started to make a move toward her goal, a little stumbling block she comes across immediately discourages her. Thoughts of her incapability to succeed at what she had barely started crawls up her spine. "I'm no good at that kind of thing; I'll just settle with this receptionist job — it is what I'm good at, and at least I get compensated for it," she'd conclude.

You see here that the problem with Grace isn't her incapability to thrive at what we wants, but discouragement when she takes a step toward her goal. She easily spots the emotion of a customer, but has failed to acknowledge her own problems. She feels emotionally insecure when she wants to take up a challenge. She thinks about the problems that she might encounter before she even starts because she doesn't want to be embarrassed or humiliated if things go south.

The Relationship Between Insecurity and Discouragement

People with emotional insecurity issues often feel discouraged. These people have low self-esteem.

They think highly of others while holding high or nonexistent expectations of themselves.

They constantly set unreachable goals, or better phrased, goals that they don't believe can come true. This is the best recipe for feeling like they are not capable of reaching them. They are too discouraged to try anything new, to develop new relationships, or even to develop new skills because they see themselves as incapable of succeeding, even before they try. They think it is easier to accept what life presents to them instead of defining what they want life to present to them and working toward it.

How to Extinguish Discouragement

The opposite of discouragement is encouragement. This is that mental state in which you make empowering affirmations, which you truly believe in, to yourself. This is the key: be credible.

If you feel deeply discouraged, vocalize small, self-encouraging statements like, "I can focus on this project for thirty minutes without interruption," or "I can take the stairs instead of the elevator every morning." What you say is who you are. Making self-encouraging statements registers encouragement in your subconscious, and with time, you'll get used to it. Saying is, however, not enough. Pay attention to the encouraging statements you make and stick to them doggedly, even if you feel discouraging powers lurking around in your brain.

Discouragement is an emotional and psychological response to the conflict between expectation and reality, which may seem to weaken the actualization of those expectations. Where there is a will, there is a way. External factors cannot help but to try to trample your goal because we don't live in an ideal world, but it is you who mustn't lessen your standard toward achieving your expectations. In fact, every discouragement should help you increase your standard of action toward meeting your expectations. Don't let discouragement turn into lethargy; let it encourage you to do more because the same influence you give discouragement is the influence it uses to quench your expectations.

Be Resilient

Wikipedia, our modern center of accessible knowledge, defines resilience as "a person's ability to successfully find a way to complete tasks facing highly adverse conditions." Resilience is a process as much as it is an ability. It is what helps an individual stick to their self-made promises, irrespective of the odds against that person.

Resilience isn't some ability that randomly occurs like the powers of the superheroes in Marvel movies. It is built by discovering your personal, unique abilities and strengths. It is when you engage in an activity or proceed with an idea that you've always thought to be unachievable that you discover your strength and ability. The knowledge of the presence of this strength in you helps you forge ahead with determination to meet your expectations.

People who become resilient slowly adopt an optimistic attitude and provoke the emotional positivity inside themselves. By practicing small encouragements repeatedly, they prove to themselves that they are able to complete whatever their minds conceive of. They only need to be realistic and willing to take action.

The first step to overcoming discouragement is to set small achievable goals that you can stick to and complete in a reasonable time.

It's a process. It takes time. In the end, you won't even know how you got there because those small achieved goals will seem like nothing individually. From that moment, you'll be convinced that you're strong enough to aim higher than you've ever dreamed of and believe that you'll actually achieve it.

Reset your focus. In those moments when you feel emotionally downcast, you can easily dwindle into melancholy, just as you'd feel great with a positive emotional feeling. Sorrow and anxiety are two very close pals that shoot one of the fiercest arrows of discouragement at achievable goals, hence attacking your emotions. They get to you worse than a bee sting, and if not properly managed, can lead to loss of focus and your own personal Waterloo, eventually.

So if you feel down because something didn't go the way you planned it, and you start hearing some discouraging chitchats in your head that says, "You're not good enough," "You won't succeed," "If you can't get past this simple step, how would you overcome the bigger ones ahead?" "You shouldn't even try," and so on, cut it out immediately. Refocus and reaffirm you self-encouragements.

Stop whatever you're doing at that moment and slowly start to feel your body's five senses. Focus on your eyes. See, don't just look. What's around you? If it helps, say out loud what you see: a car, a tree, your desk, etc. Focus on your breathing; what smells can you identify? Do the same with what you hear, touch, and taste. If you have some forbidden chocolate in your bag — just in case — this is the right time to eat it. This exercise will help you to get back into the present. It also makes you more relaxed and helps keep your anxiety or anger from escalating beyond your control.

Ditch the All-Or-Nothing Thinking

All-or-nothing thinking keeps you in the black and white color palette, not allowing you to even see gray or any other colors. It's an extreme way of thinking and very unhealthy. You set very high goals and keep your expectations at the same level as your goals without giving room for the slightest compromise. You go, "If it isn't this, then it's nothing at all," or "If it isn't perfect, then it's a failure." Like I said earlier, we don't live in an ideal world, so you should be willing to shift a bit from your white or black palette to something gray as the need arises.

Staying dogged with all-or-nothing thinking and constantly not getting all will breed weariness and discouragement in no time. When you find yourself caught up in the all-or-nothing spiral, quickly take note and warn yourself against it.

For many years, I was a prime all-or-nothing thinker. I hated it because of how it got at me, but I never found a proper method of getting over it until something extraordinary happened — *The Fifty Shades of Grey* book was published. I have to confess that it wiggled my fantasy, but not in the way you might think. Only the title.

I started using my own "fifty shades of gray" technique to combat my black and white thinking. It was a sort of punishment and encouragement from my dominant, resilient self to my unreasonable, extremist one. This may still resonate with the content of the book, but my technique offered much less pleasure.

In fact, I took a piece of paper and wrote down the numbers from one to fifty. Then I decided that I wouldn't do anything else until I found fifty gray options for my black and white problem. It was a drag. I was never able to find all the fifty solutions and fifty alternative ideas, but I found about twenty alternative ideas, which I noted. And by that time, I had so many gray ideas that I didn't hold any loyalty to the black or white idea which had led me to these alternative solutions.

I picked a random number and ended up with idea number eight. I'm fine with it. I don't care about my black or white problem anymore, just please, please don't make me think about any other solutions. I'll go crazy. It was then that I gracefully released myself from any further action of finding other alternatives.

This is a good technique for defeating all-or-nothing thinking. It brings you the best alternative results, which is also fun. It's so hilarious to have a discussion with yourself à la *Fifty Shades of Grey*, and as long as you can keep a healthy sense of humor in your life, there is no big problem. The ability to laugh at yourself is rare and cathartic.

A Six-Step Strategy to Getting Past Discouragement

Remember Grace from the beginning of this chapter? She sees the problem in her organizations' customers even before they come close to her desk. The first statement that proceeds from her mouth in reply to a customer's demand or claim melts infuriation off the customer, and yet she can't seem to help herself. Since she's not been able to help herself, let's help her get past her problem.

Realize what the problem is: All Grace aspires to be is the manager of her organization. She knows what she needs to do to get there, but she feels she can't succeed in it, maybe because of competition or her level of experience in prerequisite fields. What is her problem? She talks down to herself and thinks lowly of herself because she lacks confidence, and there's no motivation from any angle.

Define the problem. Grace now knows what her problem is, but can't pin a name to it, or maybe she doesn't want to agree to the term because she doesn't like the word. Let's help her out. DISCOURAGEMENT. That's her problem. She doesn't want to agree to the word, maybe because she's known for encouraging others.

Accept that you have the problem. Acceptance is one of the most difficult things to do. A psychopath will never admit to who he is, even though this is very important to finding solutions. Grace needs to forget about who she thinks she is and what she does well and accept that, despite the fact that she encourages her customers, she herself lacks encouragement.

Discuss with a confidant. Find a confidant that knows you well and can give you good advice. Discuss your set expectations and why you've not being able to meet them. A problem shared is half-solved, they say.

Help someone else. Truly, Grace helps people calm down or liven up, but she needs more than that. If she can help someone else with what they might need, maybe a job or a project, then she'd gain the confidence to help herself too.

Let go of the discouragement. Giving a person in need a hand gives you the feeling that you're awesome and can do almost anything. Let this kind of feeling dominate you, because if you can help someone with whatever they might need, then you can also help yourself become whatever you desire. Let go of your discouragement and connect to the accomplishing part of you.

Other Quick Tips to Overcoming Discouragement

- Break up your big goal into smaller chunks that are effortlessly achievable in small amount of time. Trying to do it all at once may bring burdening discouragements when challenges are encountered.
- Stick to the time assigned to each task as much as possible and reward yourself for every milestone successfully completed.
- Learn from your mistakes and setbacks.
- Respond to situations objectively.
- Change your routine often and make it fun.

- Talk to someone about any challenge you face along the way. Get advice from experienced people.
- Exercise and rest.

Exercises for this chapter:

1. Today I encouraged myself to make this crazy move:

   _____

2. Today I stood up for my dreams in front of:

   _____

3. Today I performed this action to start building self-confidence:

   _____

Chapter 7: Discursive Emotions

The story

Debra woke up in a good mood, which was very peculiar, because usually the best she could hope for was to wake up in a neutral one. And how lucky her inner goddess chose this day to be merciful, because today is Debra's big day. Today she will present her first individual project to the executive team of the company she works for. She is highly motivated, singing while she gets ready, wearing her bright red lipstick, and running out of her flat to the bus station and the bus that will bring her to the place of her victory.

She feels invincible. The bus comes on time and she even finds a seat. *Can this day get any better?* she thinks cheerfully. She sits down and dreamily gazes out the window. Then somebody taps her on her shoulder. It is an old man who looks at her with judgment. He says:

- "I don't know what's wrong with the youth of today, but in my day, we always offered our seats to elderly people. Clearly, you have no respect for anything. You should be ashamed of yourself, young lady. You are insensitive and selfish!"

Then the grumpy old man shuffles two rows ahead and sits down before giving Debra one more piercing look.

Debra feels like she's just become the victim of an unexpected ice bucket challenge (you know, the video challenge that circulated on Facebook last year, where people called each other out to pour buckets of ice water on their heads or donate to the ALS charity). Her good mood has been ruined. She feels that cold surprise sneaking into her stomach. Her cheeks burn. She is inundated by remorse and anger. On one hand, she feels bad for being inattentive; on the other hand, she is frustrated by the old man's condescending tone. Other seats are still empty, and anyhow, he had no right to lash out at her like that, ruining her good mood on her big day.

She starts to feel anxious about the presentation. Her good vibes have been killed, murdered by a grumpy stranger. She gets so caught up in an internal conversation where she rebukes her mood-ruiner that she forgets to get off the bus. She arrives late to her workplace, gets scolded by her boss, and feels unprofessional for making such a mistake on the day that she was supposed to be there first. Then she underperforms during her presentation.

The problem

Discursive emotions can attack those who have low or unstable self-esteem. Their emotions can fluctuate without any clear purpose. It is easy for them to bounce from one extreme to the other in just minutes. More often than not, this huge leap is caused by a minor event. Also, it's much easier for them to get from a positive extreme to a negative one than vice versa.

When people with discursive emotions feel, or just think that someone is rejecting or disapproving of them, they can take it very personally, feeling hurt, dispirited, and/or angry.

This is a peculiar way of being emotionally insecure. At one moment, people feel confident and worthy, then suddenly they take a turn when they sense a perceived or real, usually irrelevant, slight. In more severe cases, they convince themselves to be competent, only to question and berate themselves later when they've made a small mistake.

They have a tendency to catastrophize, convincing themselves that any positive state is temporary, so when they feel okay with themselves, they start ruining it by fearing future bad events that will surely ruin their present happiness. Their life is a roller coaster ride of unforeseen emotions and reactions that, in most cases, end in negativity.

The benefit of developing emotional stability

The stronger you are emotionally, the more independent you become. Not only from others' opinions, but also your own. When you know who you are and what you are capable of, you don't give such great power to any temporary external or internal stimuli.

Emotional stability doesn't mean the absence of negative thoughts, but the ability to accept them while retaining your sense of self-worth. It is the "stay tough ability" — as in S+T+Ability. Okay, that was a bad word joke, even for me. But you get the idea. When you are emotionally stable, you don't need to always be positive or boost your mood because you are sure of what matters: your strengths.

The solution

Practice how to be more emotionally stable.

1. You are not at the mercy of your emotions.

Emotions are an inevitable part of being human. Our amygdala can work in mysterious ways, as mentioned in the introduction.

However, you can get a grip on how to react on the emotions you feel. Believe it or not, if you commit to not interpreting negative events so negatively, they won't be so tough to swallow. When you find yourself feeling an emotion you don't want to feel, quickly reach out to your rational mind. "Yes, I feel sad now because of the remark of this stranger, but I won't let sadness ruin my entire day. Sadness is temporary, but the breakthrough success at my presentation at the workplace is forever," thought Debra, and went in the office to kill her presentation.

You can always choose to interpret emotionally challenging events differently — better.

If Debra kept herself in the post-bus depression, she would have ruined her presentation. She might have become irritable, pissing off her boss even more, and might have fallen even further from the promotion she's been working toward for so long.

Whenever a negative emotion overwhelms you, go back to the moment the emotion began and analyze the events rationally. If you pose some questions about the situation and answer them honestly, you'll see that there's no reason for you to feel less confident in yourself. Of course, you won't feel good about a negative incident, and you shouldn't. We're not crazy people here. Negative emotions suck. They hurt and annoy us. Embrace them, accept them, and recognize them for what they really are — a momentary brain fart in the eternal ocean of feelings. They don't affect who you are — because you are not a drop in this ocean. You are not your feelings.

2. Don't throw yourself a pity party

Fairly often, people with discursive emotions try to overcome their negative feelings by making others feel sorry for them. They hope people will say encouraging words like, "No, it was not that bad, don't worry," and so on. However, the bigger the pity party, the harder it will be to stay rational about negative emotions and overcome their malicious effect.

Emotionally stable people don't have time for pity parties because they keep their focus on their target. They don't give attention to temporary emotional disturbances — they look at the big picture.

If you have a clear target, like Debra and her presentation, put on your introspective glasses. Whenever your emotions mess with you, ask yourself: *Will this emotion help me reach my goal, or deter me from it?* Some emotions, like a mild fear or excitement, can help you push yourself more and perform better. However, in most cases, the answer is no, it won't help. You lash out, you'll feel miserable, and you won't be able to reach your target on the level you could have.

It's better to take a deep breath and compartmentalize your negative thoughts. Consider them what they are — everyday confrontations. Separate them from other fields of your life. Make sure to not let stressful life problems affect or ruin the areas that truly matter to you, like family, relationships, and work.

Imagine your life as a big wardrobe with many, many drawers. Ideally, each drawer contains different things: one has socks, the other shirts… In your life, one drawer is for your family, one for your job, and one for necessary things you must-do, like riding a bus. They are separate fields of life, but none are responsible for the others. This is why people say you should leave your work at the office instead of bringing it home. Your spouse and kids are not responsible for your evil colleague's behavior, and the boss doesn't care if your spouse was grumpy in the morning.

It's a difficult task to compartmentalize the areas of your life, but it will make your emotional life smoother and more stable. When you feel like your emotions start to rumble and become discursive, ask yourself this question: *If I give in to the effects of this event, will it help me become a better person, reach my goal, be more likable...?* Usually not.

Will this bad event change my worth? Of course not. Be mindful and stay aware of your emotions. Accept the fickle nature of emotions and consciously direct your thoughts to help you overcome the negative effects of your discursive emotions.

Exercises for this chapter:

1. Today I took responsibility for this emotional outburst I had:

   _____

2. Today I admitted myself that this event often triggers impulsive overreaction in me:

   _____

3. Today I committed to work on my shortcomings and become more emotionally stable:

_____

Chapter 8: Hypersensitivity

The story

"Let's have dinner in this newly opened restaurant. I heard they have the best lobsters," Charlie texted to his dearest's phone, attaching a link of the directions to the restaurant. He had, however, mistakenly omitted a letter before he sent it, which infuriated his wife because she though he was trying to prank her. Megan didn't text Charlie back to tell him the link was broken, and neither did she show up at the restaurant. "I won't fall prey this time," she said to herself.

Charlie and Megan has been married for over ten years now. They've been a lovely couple since they got engaged, very fond of each other and always having one another's best interests in mind. Last year was their tenth wedding anniversary, and as they've always done to celebrate, they individually planned a surprise for the other. On the anniversary eve, Megan had the top floor of their one-story duplex to herself while

Charlie chaired the ground floor, as is their custom. Usually, their anniversary mornings involved just the two of them, and later in the evenings, they'd go out to be merry with a couple friends.

On this anniversary morning, Megan had walked down in a negligée to give a special treat to her husband, who had invited his friends to reenact how he had proposed to Megan all those years ago. She was met with a big shout of "Surprise!" when the light came on. Megan was first startled, and then humiliated when she remembered what she was wearing — or rather, what she wasn't. As she scampered up the stairs, she remembered her husband had been emphasizing doing things differently.

She had become hypersensitive to any discussion or act ever since. She took everything anyone, including her husband, said personally, even general discussions. She wanted to discover the prank in every message, even when there was none, because she didn't want to be an object of humiliation a second time.

Hypersensitivity is a reaction common to people with low self-esteem and lack of confidence. They perceive insults and get their feelings hurt frequently. They get easily offended, take general statements personally, and react angrily or defensively.

When this happens, they seem insensitive to the feelings of others, and since they take everything to heart, they might also seem overly egocentric, or even narcissistic. Sometimes they seek signs of rejection from other people so they can confirm their hypersensitivity and conclude they were attacked, even when they weren't.

The following are common symptoms that suggest hypersensitivity.

They are overly self-conscious. Hypersensitive people are very cautious people. They focus on what might happen even before it does. Sometimes, with proper self-control, they can take advantage of this ability to make highly profitable decisions. As good as it may seem, it can also lead to emotional distortion in those who lack self-control.

They are often overworked. Highly sensitive people love details. They don't fancy nibbled information; they want all the information regarding any subject that's put before them. They often get overworked trying to harmonize what their less sensitive colleague has done in workplaces. They want it to be just perfect.

They attack people rather than issues and take time to make decisions. When upset, maybe because of the mistake of another person, highly sensitive people attack instead of finding a solution to the challenge. Out of emotion, they say things they don't actually mean just to satisfy their emotional disruption. No decision is trivial to them. They analyze every possibility before saying yes or no.

They tend to be lone rangers. They love to do things alone, even if a collective effort would mean speed and fun. When they have to discuss with others what they want to do, they often use the phrase, "do my thing."

With hypersensitive people, almost everything is personal. They take general statements personally, or make general statements about a specific situation. They make assumptions for one situation from other similar, or even unrelated situations. For instance, if they fail a test, they instantly conclude that they'll fail all the tests and decide to drop out of college.

Both specification and overgeneralization can lead you to have inaccurate and unhealthy beliefs about yourself. If you succeed at getting rid of them, you'll be able to reduce your emotional outbursts. You'll face less stress and be more balanced and less irritable.

Five Effective Techniques to Handle Emotional Sensitivity

1. If you want other people's compassion, be compassionate with yourself.

If you realize you acted hypersensitively (which usually comes after the storm), do not curl into a never-ending hole of guilt. Admit that you overreacted and say you're sorry if you feel you should. Take time for introspection — define what you feel, why you feel that way (something must have triggered that feeling), and think of a means to address it (could be by reminding yourself who you really are or who you aspire to be).

Overemotional and hypersensitive reactions are usually rooted in childhood or early teenage traumas. Children feel responsible for bad events that happen to them because they don't understand and can't control them. Before labeling yourself as an immature and emotionally incapable person, try to find the reasons behind your outbursts. Be compassionate with yourself and do not punish yourself with the same destructive criticism you hate so much.

2. It's not always about you.

Hypersensitive people tend to take everything personally. Even when it is not about them.

Let's say someone casually mentions that green is out of style, and you happen to wear green. How do you react? Do you even acknowledge the remark? Or do you become frustrated, ashamed, and check the validity of the statement? If you get confirmation that green was last year's color, do you throw out every single piece of green clothing you have?

If you feel attacked by this kind of comment, it means you took it personally and gave it credit. If you like green, who cares if it is in fashion or not? You need not think that person sent a hidden message to you through the comment. Just because some ill-willed fashionista says something, does that make you less of a person? No!

Learn to recover from perceived or real malicious comments, and stop taking them personally. Repeat to yourself:

"It's not about me. It's not about me. Words won't make me smaller, dumber, or less valuable. It's not about me, and it won't affect me."

3. Hypersensitivity can be an innate issue.

An article in *Psychology Today* presented that neuroscientists at the University of British Columbia have proven that our emotional sensitivity is linked to our genes, and that approximately twenty percent of the population is more sensitive than the rest. This research used Carl Jung's definition of HSP (highly sensitive person). This means an HSP has a more intense reaction to subtle stimuli. Biologically speaking, hypersensitivity is linked to a hormone called norepinephrine. This is a stress hormone that also works as a neurotransmitter to trigger attention and responses to both positive and negative events. It underlies the fight or flight response when a stressful situation is faced. [vi]

A professor at Cornell University and senior author of the study, Adam Anderson, stated, "Emotions are not only about how we feel about the world, but how our brains influence our perception of it. As our genes influence how we literally see the positive and negative aspects of our world more clearly, we may come to believe the world has more rewards or threats."

Stony Brook University's psychologist, Elaine Aron, added, "We found that areas of the brain involved with awareness and emotion, particularly those areas connected with empathetic feelings, in the highly sensitive people showed substantially greater blood flow to relevant brain areas than was seen in individuals with low sensitivity … This is physical evidence within the brain that highly sensitive individuals respond especially strongly to social situations that trigger emotions, in this case of faces being happy or sad."[vii]

So, if you've felt overly emotional all your life, you might want to dig deeper into the HSP studies to get proof that your sensitivity is indeed above average by nature.

But what can you do about it?

First, if your hypersensitivity is an inborn trait based on the aforementioned criteria, you have to learn to accept it. With practice, you can always become better and less passionately emotional in your reactions, but you might not become a person who excludes emotions from decision-making. Focus on becoming the best version of yourself, strive to explain your reactions to yourself at least, and practice minimizing how often you overreact.

How do you accept it? It can be helpful to analyze different societies and their relationships with highly sensitive individuals. In Western cultures, you are considered rather weak if you can't control your emotions, but there are other cultures where high sensitivity is considered a gift that allows you to understand other people's pain and offer comforting advice. However, this doesn't mean you shouldn't work on your sensitivity issue, especially if you sometimes feel it's nonsensical.

4. Emotional codependency

You can experience emotional codependence when you are in a relationship (romantic or any other kind of relationship, like between parent and child, between friends, etc.) where you only feel worthy and important when the other person's actions and responses give you security. You may even perceive your purpose in life as to make others happy, no matter what. Codependency can put you in an overly exposed position, where your happiness and emotional security depends on your partner's approval and actions.

Some highly sensitive people may be unconsciously codependent on their partner. They think of how they feel when their partner's action gives them security, as a way to be happy and keep the relationship blooming. It is often difficult to know when you're emotionally dependent on your partner. To know whether you're emotionally codependent on your partner, check to see if your happiness is bound to your partner's, if you make decisions based on others' wishes without considering your own benefits or wellbeing, or if you're constantly anxious about your relationship status, and when disagreements arise, you either falsely agree or become instantly defensive. If you notice one or more of these are true, then you might be more dependent on the other person than you realize.

Overcoming codependency is a greater pill to swallow, and I'd recommend consulting with a mental health professional at least a few times to get some tailor-made tips on how to start. You can also share your problems in an anonymous way with others who are in the same situation.

To get started, follow this link: http://www.coda.org. This is a codependents anonymous group where you can join face-to-face meetings all over the United States, or online meetings worldwide. If you are skeptical about the face-to-face meeting, I'd suggest trying the online version first. Whichever step you take, you should also do a little background research and participate at your own comfort level. I went to a meeting in San Francisco, and I found it very interesting.

5. The three N technique

This final technique can be applied to overcoming hypersensitive reactions as well as any other emotional insecurity. The technique itself is very simple:

- Notice it
- Name it
- Neutralize it

What does it mean to notice it? The first step to solving any problem is to discover the problem. Noticing that something is wrong is the first step to putting a bit of a distance between our rational and irrational minds. Sometimes, noticing is enough to stop an emotionally overwhelmed reaction.

However, if the first N doesn't put an end to it, you can take a further step of naming the inappropriate, overreacted, irrational, and painful behavior. For example, if you catch yourself being hypersensitive, tell yourself, "You're doing 'this' again" or "You're doing 'that' again." For, instance, if you're catastrophizing, tell yourself, "I'm being a catastrophe movie director again." Calling the devil by name and adding some humor will help you flip out of the emotional fog and see things more clearly.

Not enough? Neutralize it. How?

Engage your creative mind. Take out those thoughts that make you insecure and replace them with positive, secure thoughts. You can portray them to yourself as appropriate, say in pictures and words. It is the legacy of our brain to create pictures and subtitles of what we think all the time, like a wretched TV. If you transform the meaning of your tormenting thought into the broadcast on an old TV, which you keep hitting because it won't turn off, you've already neutralized the bad emotion and turned it into a comedy. You can imagine the soundtrack of *The Bennie Hill Show* played in the background while you struggle to make your brain-TV stop.

Benefits of Hypersensitivity

When you hear the word, "hypersensitivity," the first thought that probably crosses your mind may be the negative connotations attached to this emotional psychology. Although being highly sensitive may mean all those things a person would like change, it also has positive sides.

Highly sensitive people are usually good communicators. They infer from actions and see beyond a statement made. They visualize different possibilities that may be associated with an idea or a comment, and know where to focus for more elaborate information. Functionally sensitive people are known to be organized, reflective, empathetic, and motivated to succeed.

Apart from being good communicators, emotionally sensitive people are known for honesty and consistency. They say things exactly the way they are, sharply and bluntly. They share experiences as naturally as they are and put meaning into every act.

Hypersensitive people connect with life and absorb all its virtue. They rarely get bored because they attach meaning and seriousness to whatever they do, even when it may seem otherwise for less-sensitive individuals. As an emotionally sensitive person, you see reasons behind everything and you accept, which makes you free.

Hypersensitivity means being able to perceive and feel emotions with intensity. Your empathy is on a different level from others', always wanting to offer help even when the best response is no. You feel passionately, never wanting to let go.

By now, you can see that emotional sensitivity can be just as much a blessing as a curse. Those who harness the beauty and constructive aspect of hypersensitivity turn out to be successful people. You don't have to eradicate your sensitivity, you just have to pick those traits that aren't healthy for you to analyze and neutralize them as appropriate.

Let the few techniques outlined in this chapter help you control your emotional sensitivity while keeping your head up to the positivity attached to this psychological influence.

Exercises for this chapter:

1. Today I caught myself before acting hypersensitively about this topic:

   _____

2. Today I made this step to learn to control my hypersensitive outbursts:

   _____

3. Today I understood why my partner acts so emotionally to this topic. In the future, I'll try to bring it up differently:

The topic: The changed approach:

_____

Closing Thoughts

If you're reading these lines, it means you read all the chapters about the different types of emotional insecurities, their causes, the benefits you gain from controlling them, and solutions on how to gain control.

Stop reading for a moment, and notice what your thoughts are right now. What do you think about the concepts you just read? What are the emotional insecurities you could relate to? What emotional insecurities could you not relate to at all? Which ones made you anxious, angry, or sad?

Examine your thoughts and feelings. When you read a book like this, it is important to stop and see where your mind wanders — the more often you stop and listen to your internal voice, the more you'll learn about yourself. In the long run, this will prove very useful.

You are free to think whatever you like. You can say this book was very good and informative, or it was total crap. You can agree or disagree with me. What matters is that you make honest remarks, and if you accept that something is painful, be honest with yourself. There's no change without pain.

If you could relate to some of the emotional insecurities presented in the book, pick a maximum of two of them and start working on improving in those areas. You can take my advice. If you don't like it, or you feel you need another perspective, just do more research on the insecurity in question and find solutions that resonate better with you. If my book only helped you with the identification of your insecurity, I'm already satisfied.

Don't work on more than two issues at a time. Choose the most important, urgent, or disturbing ones and start getting over them. Even if it is tempting, do not commit to more than two, because you'll divide your focus and end up achieving nothing.

Patience, resilience, and commitment. This is all you need in your pocket. And some M&Ms, the equivalent of Popeye's spinach.

Work a little bit each day on your insecurities, and you'll find that hard work makes you stronger than the day before. Follow the guidance you choose on how to overcome your problem, take time to examine your thoughts, and set your emotions free.

This is a big world. None of us are identical; we all have differences. It's unavoidable. This is why we should do our best not to be affected by differing opinions, because if we do, we'll be affected at every corner.

Remember, people with high self-confidence make a lot of mistakes just like anyone else, but unlike others, they don't let these mistakes take over their attitude. Mistakes and failures become the main source of feedback that helps them readjust their actions.

Living a bit outside of your head can be helpful. Are you one of those people who occasionally or always expect negative outcomes? There is no magical one-sentence formula for how to stop catastrophe creation — you simply have to commit to stop doing it.

Your emotions don't reflect reality, but the way you choose to interpret reality. If you accept this, you'll be able to get almost total control over your emotions.

Emotional strength allows you to focus on being able to do what you love instead of constantly avoiding what you hate. People who become resilient slowly adopt an optimistic attitude. By practicing small encouragements repeatedly, they prove to themselves they are able to complete whatever their minds conceive of. Therefore, they effectively balance negative emotions with positive ones.

Emotional stability doesn't mean the absence of negative thoughts, but the ability to not lose your sense of self-worth. Both specification and overgeneralization can lead you to having inaccurate and unhealthy beliefs about yourself. If you succeed at getting rid of them, you'll be able to reduce your emotional outbursts to a smaller amplitude. You'll face less stress, and you'll be more balanced and less irritable.

I hope this empowering summary can help you get up, take a deep breath, and take the first step on your journey to emotional strength. Your destiny is in your hands.

I believe in you!

Yours truly,

Zoe

Reference

Bergland, Christopher. *How Do Your Genes Influence Levels of Emotional Sensitivity?* Psychology Today. 2015.
https://www.psychologytoday.com/blog/the-athletes-way/201505/how-do-your-genes-influence-levels-emotional-sensitivity

Burton, Neel. *The Psychology of Humiliation.* Psychology Today. 2014.
https://www.psychologytoday.com/blog/hide-and-seek/201408/the-psychology-humiliation

Harris, Russ. *The Confidence Gap*. Trumpeter. 2011.

Hayes, Steven C. Strosahl, Kirk D. Wilson, Kelly G. *Acceptance and Commitment Therapy: An Experimental Approach to Behavior Change.* The Guilford Press. 2003.

Khoo, Nina. *How Science can help us see the Highly Sensitive Trait in a Positive Light.* Nina Khoo. 2017. http://ninakhoo.com/project/car-connect-9/

Krauss Whitbourne, Susan, Ph.D. Susan Krauss Whitbourne Ph.D. *4 Signs That Someone Is Probably Insecure*. Psychology Today. 2015. https://www.psychologytoday.com/blog/fulfillment-any-age/201511/4-signs-someone-is-probably-insecure

Scherer, Klaus. *Appraisal Processes in Emotion: Theory, Methods, Research (Series in Affective Science)*. Oxford University Press. 2001.

Endnotes

[i] Scherer, Klaus. *Appraisal Processes in Emotion: Theory, Methods, Research (Series in Affective Science).* Oxford University Press. 2001.
[ii] Harris, Russ. *The Confidence Gap.* Trumpeter. 2011.
[iii] Hayes, Steven C. Strosahl, Kirk D. Wilson, Kelly G. *Acceptance and Commitment Therapy: An Experimental Approach to Behavior Change.* The Guilford Press. 2003.
[iv] Krauss Whitbourne, Susan, Ph.D. Susan Krauss Whitbourne Ph.D. *4 Signs That Someone Is Probably Insecure.* Psychology Today. 2015. https://www.psychologytoday.com/blog/fulfillment-any-age/201511/4-signs-someone-is-probably-insecure
[v] Burton, Neel. *The Psychology of Humiliation.* Psychology Today. 2014. https://www.psychologytoday.com/blog/hide-and-seek/201408/the-psychology-humiliation
[vi] Bergland, Christopher. *How Do Your Genes Influence Levels of Emotional Sensitivity?* Psychology Today. 2015. https://www.psychologytoday.com/blog/the-

athletes-way/201505/how-do-your-genes-influence-levels-emotional-sensitivity

[vii] Khoo, Nina. *How Science can help us see the Highly Sensitive Trait in a Positive Light.* Nina Khoo. 2017. http://ninakhoo.com/project/car-connect-9/

Made in the USA
San Bernardino, CA
07 February 2018